GROUND BREAKERS
BLACK MOVIE MAKERS

OSCAR MICHEAUX

by Joyce Markovics
and Alrick A. Brown

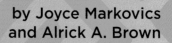

CHERRY LAKE PRESS
cherrylakepublishing.com

Published in the United States of America by Cherry Lake Publishing Group
Ann Arbor, Michigan
www.cherrylakepublishing.com

Reading Adviser: Beth Walker Gambro, MS, Ed., Reading Consultant, Yorkville, IL
Content Adviser: Alrick A. Brown, Film Professor and Filmmaker
Book Designer: Ed Morgan

Photo Credits: Everett Collection/Alamy Stock Photo, cover and title page; Wikimedia Commons, 5; Wikimedia Commons, 6; Wikimedia Commons, 7; Wikimedia Commons, 8; Library of Congress, Prints & Photographs Division, Farm Security Administration/Office of War Information Black-and-White Negatives, 9; Library of Congress, Prints & Photographs Division, 10; Public Domain, 11; Schomburg Center for Research in Black Culture, Photographs and Prints Division, The New York Public Library, 12; Wikimedia Commons, 13; Wikimedia Commons, 14; Public Domain, 15; Public Domain, 16; Public Domain, 17; Wikimedia Commons, 18; AFI/Filmoteca Espanola Collection (Library Of Congress), 19; Public Domain, 21.

Library of Congress Cataloging-in-Publication Data has been filed and is available at catalog.loc.gov.

Printed in the United States of America by
Corporate Graphics

CONTENTS

THIS IS OSCAR

> "YOUR SELF IMAGE IS SO POWERFUL IT BECOMES YOUR DESTINY."
> —OSCAR MICHEAUX

Filmmaker Oscar Micheaux (1884–1951) shattered barriers. He wrote, produced, and directed 44 movies at a time when Black Americans faced extreme **racism**. He not only addressed racism, inequality, and other issues in his films, he celebrated the lives of Black people. Nearly 100 years after his death, Oscar's movies have left a rich **legacy**. Yet few people know about this groundbreaking moviemaker.

Oscar Micheaux made both silent films and films with sound.

Oscar Micheaux was also a successful author. He published at least seven books and likely many more.

EARLY LIFE

On January 2, 1884, Oscar Micheaux was born on a farm near Metropolis, Illinois, to parents Calvin and Bell. He was the 5th of 11 children. Both of Oscar's parents were born into slavery in Kentucky. They settled in the North to build a better life for their family. Still, life was a struggle. They farmed their land, hunted, and fished to sustain themselves. They valued education, yet neither parent could read or write. Bell idolized the great Black educator Booker T. Washington and taught her children about him.

Booker T. Washington was born in 1856 and died in 1915. He championed racial equality.

Oscar grew up quoting Booker T. Washington. One of his favorite quotes was, "It is at the bottom of life we should begin and not at the top. Nor should we permit our grievances to overshadow our opportunities."

Oscar's last name comes from the Kentucky slave owner who enslaved his father's family.

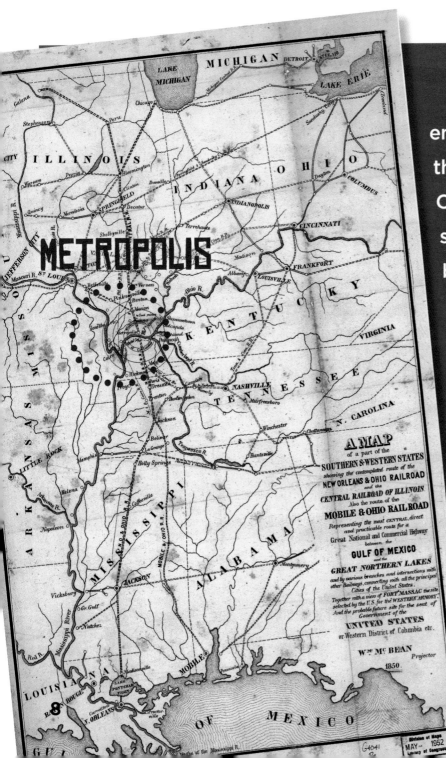

Bell and Calvin saved enough money to send their children to school. Oscar described his school as "an old building of plain boards." Even though it was run down and "inadequate" according to Oscar, he quickly learned to read and write. In class, Oscar often got in trouble for talking too much and asking too many questions.

Metropolis, Illinois

To make extra money on the weekends, Oscar sold his family's farm goods at the local market. He had an obvious talent for sales and connecting with people. These skills would help him later in life.

Thinking he had learned all he could from school, Oscar dropped out. At age 17, he moved to Chicago. While living with his older brother, Oscar worked many odd jobs. He soon became fed up with the work and how little he earned. Frustrated, Oscar decided to become his own boss. He started a shoeshine stand in a barbershop for wealthy Black men. Oscar learned about running a business and started to earn enough money to save. From there, he worked as a Pullman porter. This job allowed Oscar to save even more money, see the country, and meet many different kinds of people.

A young shoeshiner in 1899

A Pullman porter at work

Pullman porters carried bags, shined shoes, and set up sleeping quarters for passengers. At the time, being a Pullman porter was one of the best and highest-paying jobs available to Black men.

With the money Oscar earned as a porter, he bought land in South Dakota. Oscar cultivated more land than any of his white neighbors in the first year. Oscar got married, but the relationship fell apart. To deal with his hardships, Oscar began writing about his experiences. Soon, he had written an entire novel called *The Conquest: The Story of a Negro Pioneer*. Not long after, he wrote another book, *The Homesteader*. A movie company approached Oscar about making it into a film. But Oscar wanted to tell his own story. So, he adapted the book into his first movie.

Oscar Micheaux in 1919, the year *The Homesteader* was released.

"THERE IS NO BARRIER TO SUCCESS WHICH DILIGENCE AND PERSEVERANCE CANNOT HURDLE."
—OSCAR MICHEAUX

Oscar was one of the first Black Americans to write and direct a feature film.

MAKING MOVIES

Oscar founded the Micheaux Film & Book Company. His first project was filming *The Homesteader*, a silent movie released in 1919. It was a drama about a man not unlike himself. In addition, the movie was a love story that brought up issues of race. Black audiences loved it. **Critics** raved about it. The movie launched Oscar's filmmaking career.

Evelyn Preer played a main character in *The Homesteader*. She is considered to be the first Black female movie star.

Many other movies followed. Oscar's film *Within Our Gates* from 1920 has a racist white man as one of the main characters. The racist changes his ways when he realizes the Black woman he is about to attack is his own daughter. Oscar's films often thoughtfully combined the subjects of race, love, and drama.

A still image from Oscar's *Within Our Gates*

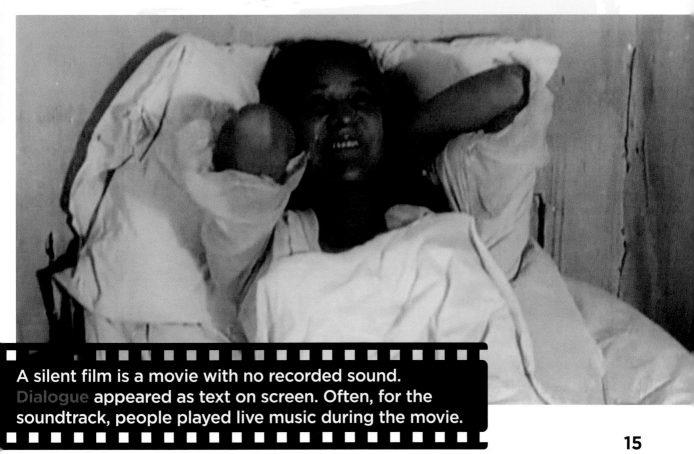

A silent film is a movie with no recorded sound. Dialogue appeared as text on screen. Often, for the soundtrack, people played live music during the movie.

Oscar was not afraid to show lynchings and other violence against Black people in his films. He wanted his movies to reflect what was happening in the country. He didn't just show African Americans as victims, however. He included Black doctors, lawyers, and business owners in his films too. It was Oscar's way to speak up against racism and inequality.

"WHAT I LIKE BEST IS A GOOD STORY WITH A MORAL."
—OSCAR MICHEAUX

Paul Robeson was a famous Black singer, actor, athlete, and activist. Oscar hired him to star in his silent film *Body and Soul* (1925).

Paul Robeson in *Body and Soul*

In the late 1920s, movies with sound became more popular. Oscar tried to compete against big movie studios. But he struggled. Oscar married actress Alice B. Russell, who became his partner in life and business. They settled down in Harlem. He focused on writing novels.

In 1948, Oscar released his final film, *The Betrayal*. It was a flop. Then Oscar's health began to fail. In March 1951, it's thought that Oscar traveled to the South to promote his books. On March 25, he died from his illnesses. Oscar was just 67 years old.

GREATEST NEGRO PHOTOPLAY OF ALL TIME

ASTOR PICTURES Presents

The Betrayal

OSCAR MICHEAUX'S
Thrilling Motion Picture Epic

Based on the immortal novel
"THE WIND FROM NOWHERE"

"HONEST, INTELLIGENT CRITICISM IS AN AID TO THE PROGRESS OF AN EFFORT."
—OSCAR MICHEAUX

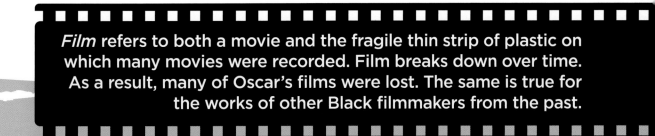

Film refers to both a movie and the fragile thin strip of plastic on which many movies were recorded. Film breaks down over time. As a result, many of Oscar's films were lost. The same is true for the works of other Black filmmakers from the past.

Over 30 years, Oscar made an astounding 40 movies. Many were made on a tiny budget. However, all had a big impact. "I really think he was one of the greatest filmmakers of the silent era," said Charles Musser, a film professor and historian.

An image from one of Oscar's many feature films

OSCAR'S IMPACT

Oscar's movies were like windows into the lives of Black Americans. He once said, "It is only by presenting those portions of the race portrayed in my pictures, in the light and background of their true state, that we can raise our people to greater heights." The groundbreaking and prolific filmmaker Oscar Micheaux kept his passion. He never gave up his fight for justice and equality. His gravestone aptly reads, "A Man Ahead of His Time."

Oscar received a Director's Guild of America special award for his work more than 30 years after his death.

FILMOGRAPHY

Year	Title		Year	Title
1919	*The Homesteader*		1929	*The Wages of Sin*
1920	*Within Our Gates*		1930	*Easy Street*
1920	*The Brute*		1930	*A Daughter of the Congo*
1920	*The Symbol of the Unconquered*		1931	*Darktown Revue*
1921	*The Gunsaulus Mystery*		1931	*The Exile*
1922	*The Dungeon*		1932	*Veiled Aristocrats*
1922	*The Hypocrite*		1932	*Ten Minutes to Live*
1922	*Uncle Jasper's Will*		1932	*Black Magic*
1922	*The Virgin of the Seminole*		1932	*The Girl from Chicago*
1923	*Deceit*		1933	*Ten Minutes to Kill*
1924	*Birthright*		1933	*Phantom of Kenwood*
1924	*A Son of Satan*		1934	*Harlem After Midnight*
1925	*Body and Soul*		1935	*Murder in Harlem*
1925	*Marcus Garland*		1936	*Temptation*
1926	*The Conjure Woman*		1937	*Underworld*
1926	*The Devil's Disciple*		1938	*God's Step Children*
1926	*The Spider's Web*		1938	*Swing!*
1927	*The Millionaire*		1939	*Lying Lips*
1927	*The House Behind the Cedars*		1939	*Birthright*
1928	*The Broken Violin*		1940	*The Notorious Elinor Lee*
1928	*Thirty Years Later*		1948	*The Betrayal*
1929	*When Men Betray*			